Scaling Machine Learning

Industrializing ML with MLOps and Automation

Taylor Royce

DEDICATION

To all the engineers, data scientists, and innovators who work to expand the realm of machine learning's potential. We are all inspired by your unwavering commitment to excellence and your use of technology. On your quest to turn concepts into meaningful solutions, may this book act as a roadmap and a source of motivation.

To my friends and family, whose constant encouragement and support have stoked my enthusiasm for this area. I appreciate your confidence in me and your unwavering support.

And to the next generation of creators and thinkers: may your bravery and vision continue to lead you to explore, invent, and change the world.

CONTENTS

ACKNOWLEDGMENTS

To everyone who helped create and finish *Scaling Machine Learning: Industrializing ML with MLOps and Automation*, I would like to extend my sincere gratitude.

I want to start by expressing my gratitude to my mentors and coworkers, whose knowledge and experience have greatly impacted my comprehension of machine learning and its industrial applications. The concepts given in this book have been greatly influenced by your advice.

My research partners and peers, who participated in thought-provoking conversations, shared their experiences, and offered helpful criticism during the writing process, have my sincere gratitude. This effort was greatly enhanced by your cooperation and assistance.

Additionally, I would like to thank the efforts of the larger machine learning community, whose ongoing innovation and commitment to knowledge-sharing motivate both practitioners and students. The information in this book has been greatly influenced by the sources, papers, and conversations.

I want to express my gratitude to my family and friends for their support, tolerance, and understanding over the many hours I spent writing. Your steadfast support of my vision has given me courage and inspiration.

Lastly, I want to thank all of the people who have read this book. Your quest for knowledge and dedication to developing machine learning inspire me to impart my knowledge and promote a better comprehension of this ever-evolving field. I hope you find this book to be a useful tool for your trip.

CHAPTER 1

GETTING TO KNOW INDUSTRIALIZED MACHINE LEARNING

1.1 Industrialized Machine Learning Definition

An important development in the use of machine learning (ML) technologies is industrialized machine learning. Industrialized machine learning (ML) aims to scale and standardize machine learning applications across businesses, allowing them to tackle difficult, large-scale challenges, in contrast to traditional ML approaches that are frequently restricted to experimental or academic settings.

- **From Specialty to Need:** From a specialized area of computer science, machine learning has quickly developed into a key technology transforming industries including manufacturing, e-commerce, healthcare, and finance. The majority of early machine learning applications were experimental, with little practical implementation. However, industries now depend more and more on machine learning (ML) to improve decision-making, streamline operations, and develop new services, underscoring the need for reliable, industrialized ML systems.

Features of Industrialized Machine Learning:

Operational scalability, consistency, and dependability across a range of business applications are key components of industrialized machine learning. Important traits consist of:

- **Automation:** Processes are streamlined by automated data pipelines, model training, and model deployment, which minimizes human involvement and shortens production time.

- **Standardization:** By enforcing best practices and defined techniques, industrialized machine learning enables repeatable, predictable outcomes across deployments.

- **Business Workflow Integration:** In industrialized environments, machine learning models are integrated directly with enterprise systems rather than being in separate silos, which improves their capacity to deliver actionable insights.

Advantages for Organizations:

- **Enhanced Efficiency:** Automated machine learning procedures enable businesses to grow their operations effectively, enabling large-scale implementation of intricate activities like fraud detection, predictive maintenance, and personalization.

- **Improved Consistency:** Industrialized machine learning makes outputs more stable and consistent by lowering model performance variability.

- **Accelerated Innovation:** Businesses may experiment and iterate more quickly with the automation of machine learning processes, resulting in the quicker release of new features and products.

1.2 Development of Experimental to Production Machine Learning

From its beginnings as a strictly academic and experimental discipline to its current position as a fundamental component of industrial technology, machine learning has experienced a profound transformation. This move from experimental to production machine learning required a number of significant adjustments to methods, tools, and mentality.

Experimental Machine Learning: The Initial Phase: At first, machine learning models were frequently limited to laboratory settings and prioritized theoretical validation over real-world implementation. To assess model correctness, data scientists and researchers would conduct experiments, frequently managing training procedures and manually selecting datasets. Few models survived past the research stage, and these early stages were marked by limited scalability.

Production ML: Scaling for Practical Applications:

Accessibility and Volume of Data: The range of ML applications grew as businesses started to produce enormous volumes of data. Big data's accessibility served as the catalyst for the development of increasingly intricate and precise models.

Infrastructure Advancements: Distributed processing and cloud computing enabled ML algorithms to process larger datasets and carry out more intricate calculations. The ability to move ML models from prototypes to systems that are suitable for production depends heavily on infrastructure.

Lifecycle Management Model: Systematic management of the model, including training, implementation, monitoring, and upgrading, became necessary. In order to help enterprises transition from a research-centric approach to operational production environments, tools such as MLflow, Kubeflow, and TensorFlow Extended (TFX) made it easier to manage ML lifecycles.

MLOps Practice Development: By incorporating automation, monitoring, and collaborative development into ML workflows, MLOps concepts borrowed from DevOps. This change made it possible for teams to constantly manage models in production, guaranteeing their accuracy and continued applicability.

Production ML Challenges:

- **Data Drift:** Model performance may deteriorate as a result of production machine learning's need to take into account shifting data patterns over time.

- **Retraining and updating the model:** Maintaining model correctness requires regular retraining, which calls for reliable procedures for recognizing and reacting to update requirements.

- **Interdisciplinary Collaboration:** Data scientists, engineers, and domain specialists must work together to deploy machine learning at scale, which promotes a more integrated approach to problem-solving.

1.3 Industrialization's Contribution to ML Scaling

The ability of ML systems to scale across various domains and applications is made possible by industrialization, which successfully elevates ML from discrete, small-scale initiatives to the center of organizational strategy. Industrialization makes it possible to apply machine learning (ML) at previously unheard-of scales, revolutionizing procedures and facilitating quick, data-driven decision-making.

The following are standard workflows to ensure consistency: Workflows are standardized by industrialized machine learning, which guarantees consistency across models even when used to address various business issues. Data preprocessing, feature engineering, model training, and evaluation are all covered by standardization, which produces dependable, reproducible results.

Key ML Processes Are Automated: To handle the intricacy of ML pipelines on an industrial scale, automation is crucial. Systems for industrialized machine learning:

- **Select and tune models automatically:** Model selection, hyperparameter tuning, and other processes that formerly needed a lot of manual input are made easier by automated machine learning (AutoML) systems.

- In order to facilitate faster model changes and reduce downtime in production systems, MLOps frameworks integrate Continuous Integration and Deployment (CI/CD) for machine learning.

Scalability in a Variety of Applications: Industrialized machine learning may enable a wide range of applications by offering scalable infrastructure, including:

- **Healthcare:** Deploying models that support diagnostics, predictive analytics, and individualized treatment—all of which call for strict performance and regulatory requirements—is part of scaling machine learning in the healthcare industry.

- **Finance:** Large datasets can be analyzed in real time

by industrialized machine learning in the finance industry to identify fraud, control risks, and customize consumer experiences.

- **The manufacturing process:** Manufacturers can reduce downtime, streamline supply chains, and boost operational efficiency with the use of machine learning-powered predictive maintenance.

Facilitating Instantaneous Decision-Making: Many applications require the ability to make decisions in real time, particularly in industries like finance and e-commerce. This is accomplished by industrialized ML systems by:

- **Processing Data in Real Time:** Models are able to process data as it comes in, giving quick insights that can be used right away.

- **Streamlined Model Deployment:** Production-ready models are swiftly implemented in various contexts, guaranteeing that machine learning systems can react to fresh data with the least amount of lag.

Maintenance and Monitoring: To guarantee that models operate consistently and provide trustworthy insights, industrialized machine learning necessitates extensive monitoring mechanisms. Monitoring consists of:

- **Tracking Model Performance:** Teams can identify and address problems such as data drift or decreased accuracy with real-time feedback on model performance.

- **Automated Warnings and Modifications**: Automated warnings can be used to inform teams or start retraining processes when models deteriorate, guaranteeing that models continue to be accurate and functioning over time.

- **Compliance and Governance:** To ensure accountability, transparency, and data protection in regulated businesses, industrialized machine learning systems must follow governance and compliance norms.

Organizations may fully utilize machine learning at scale through industrialization, which formalizes and standardizes ML processes. Industrialized machine learning has created new opportunities and made it possible for ML to drive strategic growth, efficiency, and innovation in almost every industry.

CHAPTER 2

BUILDING THE INDUSTRIALIZED ML PIPELINE

For raw data to be transformed into actionable insights that support large-scale decision-making, an efficient machine learning pipeline must be established. From data collection to model deployment, the industrialized ML pipeline optimizes procedures, guaranteeing accuracy, consistency, and efficiency in machine learning applications across a range of domains.

2.1 Pipelines for Data Collection and Preprocessing

Any effective machine learning project starts with a clearly defined pipeline for data gathering and preprocessing. To ensure consistent model performance, industrialized machine learning depends on reliable, automated procedures that manage data intake, cleaning, and preparation at scale.

Data Collection Techniques: To manage vast amounts and types of data in an industrialized environment, data collection needs to be scalable, secure, and dependable. **Typical methods include:**

- Real-time data streaming from several sources is made possible by APIs and Webhooks:, providing dependable and rapid access to the most recent data.

- For applications that don't need real-time insights, batch processing which is used for high-volume data sources allows data to be collected at predetermined intervals for bulk analysis.

- **Streaming Data Pipelines:** Streaming data pipelines (like Apache Kafka or AWS Kinesis) provide real-time processing of continuously flowing data for applications like fraud detection or real-time suggestions.

Data Preprocessing Strategies: The dependability of machine learning models is directly impacted by the caliber of input data. In industrialized machine learning, preprocessing techniques guarantee data consistency and integrity by:

- Removing or fixing errors, dealing with missing

numbers, and resolving discrepancies within datasets are all examples of data cleaning. This covers methods such as outlier elimination and imputation (estimating missing values).

- **Normalization and Standardization:** It is important to make sure that all data values are on the same scale, particularly for machine learning models like neural networks that are sensitive to numerical magnitude.

The creation of pertinent input features that improve model correctness is known as "feature engineering." In industrialized machine learning pipelines, feature engineering frequently involves methods like as

- The process of transforming categorical data into a binary format appropriate for models is known as "one-hot encoding."
- **Dimensionality Reduction:** To maximize computing efficiency, methods such as Principal Component Analysis (PCA) minimize feature dimensions while preserving crucial information.
- **Time-Series Conversion:** Preprocessing for temporal data can include seasonally correcting, detrending, or consolidating the data.

Monitoring the Quality of Data:

To maintain model reliability over time, data quality monitoring is essential. Data quality tests like schema validation and anomaly detection are frequently included in industrialized machine learning processes to identify problems in the data that could impair model performance.

2.2 Workflows for Training and Validation

Workflows for training and validation need to be scalable, effective, and automated in order to satisfy the expectations of industrialized machine learning. These methods facilitate iterative experimentation for ongoing development and convert preprocessed data into high-performing models that are prepared for deployment.

Automated Training Pipelines: To reduce human intervention, speed up model training, and simplify experimentation, industrialized machine learning makes use of automated training pipelines. Important elements consist of:

- **Data Splitting Automation:** Models are guaranteed

to generalize effectively on unseen data when data is consistently divided into training, validation, and testing sets. Automation increases the robustness of the model by lowering the chance of data leakage.

- **Hyperparameter tweaking:** By employing techniques such as grid search, random search, or Bayesian optimization, automated hyperparameter optimization allows for quicker and more efficient model tweaking, which enhances performance.

- **Distributed Training:** Using frameworks such as TensorFlow, PyTorch, or Spark, distributed training can help expand computation across numerous computers and cut down on training time for huge datasets.

Model Validation Techniques: Prior to deployment, validation is necessary to determine whether ML models are generalizable. Industrialized pipelines employ a number of techniques to guarantee dependable operation:

- The process of **cross-validation:** divides data into several subsets in order to assess the consistency of the model across various data segments. Commonly employed methods include K-fold cross-validation.

- By designating a subset of the dataset as a validation set, **Hold-Out Validation:** allows for an objective evaluation of the model's performance.

- **Real-Time Validation:** Real-time validation, also known as online validation, assesses model accuracy on fresh, incoming data for applications that need dynamic model updates.

Experiment Tracking and Management: To support auditability, cooperation, and reproducibility, industrialized machine learning requires comprehensive documentation of training trials. To support ongoing model optimization, data scientists can record and review experiment parameters, hyperparameters, and outcomes using experiment-tracking tools (like MLflow, Weights & Biases, or DVC).

2.3 Production Deployment and Monitoring

Deployment is the start of ongoing monitoring and development in industrialized machine learning, which guarantees that models continue to be efficient and in line with corporate objectives. In order to sustain model performance over time, production pipelines place a high priority on smooth deployment, real-time monitoring, and feedback loops.

- **Model Deployment Techniques:** Strategies for deployment range from batch processing to real-time inferencing, depending on the needs of the application.
- **Deployment in Batch:** Batch deployment is appropriate for processing data on a regular basis (e.g., weekly or daily). Applications such as quarterly financial modeling or sales forecasting are best suited for batch deployment.
- **Deployment in Real Time:** Real-time deployment uses REST APIs or microservices to make models available in real-time for applications that need predictions right away. Fast processing is made possible by low-latency frameworks like TensorFlow Serving or FastAPI.
- **Deployment A/B Testing:** A/B testing enables data-driven deployment decisions by comparing several model versions in production and evaluating performance on actual user interactions.

Model Monitoring and Maintenance: Keeping an eye on models is essential to making sure they keep functioning well in the changing situations they are used in. Monitoring includes:

- In order to identify performance degradation, performance parameters such as accuracy, precision, recall, and response time are continuously evaluated.

- **Detection of Data Drift:** Model performance may suffer from data drift as real-world data changes. Methods like distribution-based approaches or statistical tests are used to identify changes in the distributions of input data.

- **Retraining and updating the model:** In order to ensure that models are regularly updated to reflect new data patterns, industrialized machine learning systems incorporate automated retraining methods that are triggered by data drift or performance deterioration.

Feedback Loops for Continuous Improvement: Feedback loops are a feature of industrialized machine learning pipelines that allow models to be improved through user interactions or system outputs. This is especially useful in contexts like tailored suggestions where model accuracy increases with each iteration.

- **User Feedback Integration:** Gathering user feedback (such as clicks, likes, and ratings) aids in modifying models according to user preferences and patterns of activity.

- **Error Logging and Analysis:** Finding misclassifications or outliers helps to inform the retraining process by revealing areas where models can be improved.

Organizations build resilient machine learning pipelines that enable consistent performance in production settings by putting in place strong deployment, monitoring, and feedback loops. These procedures guarantee that models not only produce accurate results but also adjust to changing user requirements and data, resulting in significant business outcomes.

CHAPTER 3

INDUSTRIAL ML SOFTWARE INFRASTRUCTURE

For ML workflows to be scalable, dependable, and repeatable, the software infrastructure supporting industrial machine learning is essential. In order to handle the complexity and size of contemporary machine learning projects, this infrastructure must be built using cloud computing, containerization, orchestration, and automation technologies. These elements serve as the foundation for effective machine learning implementation, facilitating quicker time to market and reliable model management in manufacturing.

3.1 ML Operations with Cloud Computing (MLOps)

Because cloud computing and ML Operations (MLOps) provide scalable, adaptable, and effective infrastructure, they have revolutionized the development, deployment, and maintenance of ML projects. While cloud platforms offer on-demand access to robust computational resources, MLOps concentrates on the full machine learning lifecycle, guaranteeing that models are created with scalability and operational stability.

Cloud Infrastructure's Function in ML Scaling:

Because it allows businesses to modify resources according to project needs, cloud computing offers the scalable infrastructure needed for industrial machine learning. Important advantages include:

- **Elasticity:** By preventing idle infrastructure, cloud platforms enable businesses to scale resources up or down in response to changing demands, which lowers expenses.

- **Data Storage and Management:** Cloud service providers such as AWS, Google Cloud, and Azure provide ML-optimized storage solutions, including database options for structured data and object storage for unstructured data.

- **Computing Power for Training and Inference:** The cloud makes it possible to utilize potent GPUs and TPUs (Tensor Processing Units) for quicker machine learning model training. This is especially helpful for large, deep learning models that need a lot of calculations.

The Effect of MLOps on ML Lifecycle Management:

MLOps is a collection of procedures that improve model traceability and reliability by integrating DevOps concepts into the machine learning lifecycle. MLOps addresses a number of important topics:

- **Versioning the Model:** Iterative reproduction, testing, and improvement of models are ensured by maintaining track of various model versions. Model version control is made easier by tools like MLflow and DVC (Data Version Control), which allow for smooth model iteration.

- **Experiment monitoring:** Data scientists can keep an eye on model performance metrics, hyperparameters, and results across iterations thanks to MLOps platforms' centralized monitoring for model experiments.

- **Continuous Deployment/Continuous Integration (CI/CD):** By automating model testing, validation, and deployment, CI/CD pipelines may be implemented in MLOps, which decreases manual involvement and speeds up deployment.

Cloud-Based MLOps Solutions: To make managing ML infrastructure easier, numerous cloud platforms provide integrated MLOps solutions:

- With tools for data preparation, training, deployment, and monitoring, Google Cloud Vertex AI facilitates end-to-end ML lifecycle management.
- In an integrated context, Azure Machine Learning provides MLOps features, such as model training, deployment, and monitoring.
- With features like SageMaker Pipelines for MLOps automation, AWS SageMaker offers tools for model construction, training, and deployment.

3.2 Tools for Orchestration and Containerization

Containerization and orchestration technologies in industrial machine learning (ML) make it easier to create, implement, and scale models in many contexts. Consistency is made possible by containers, and scalable management of these containers by orchestration technologies guarantees dependable and seamless operations.

Docker is a widely used containerization solution that ensures consistency from development to production by encapsulating applications and their dependencies in isolated environments. Advantages consist of:

- **Environment Consistency**: Docker containers avoid inconsistencies between development and production environments by packaging code, dependencies, and configurations.

- **Portability and Scalability:** ML applications may be easily scaled horizontally by deploying Docker containers on any system that supports Docker.

- **Simplified Model Deployment:** By minimizing dependency conflicts and guaranteeing that models operate dependably regardless of the underlying infrastructure, containers make model deployment easier.

Kubernetes-based orchestration:

An orchestration tool called Kubernetes was created to scale containerized application management. It is crucial for large-scale machine learning operations because it simplifies the deployment, scaling, and management of containerized applications. Among Kubernetes' salient features are:

- **Automated Scaling:** Kubernetes ensures effective resource use by automatically scaling containers up or down to suit demand.

- **Service Discovery and Load Balancing:** In order to balance workloads, Kubernetes divides network traffic among containers, guaranteeing high availability and effective model inference request processing.

- **Rolling Rollbacks and Updates:** Model deployment updates are made possible by Kubernetes' smooth container updates, which eliminate downtime. In order to maintain continuity, it also permits rolling back to earlier container versions in the event of failures.

Using Docker and Kubernetes Together for ML: Using Docker and Kubernetes together offers a comprehensive approach to ML model deployment in production settings:

- **Dockerized ML Models:** Data scientists ensure that each model has a reproducible environment by containerizing models using Docker.

- **Orchestrated Deployment with Kubernetes:** After these models are containerized, Kubernetes controls their deployment, scaling, and lifespan in production, enabling industrial-scale machine learning with little manual involvement.

Tools for Orchestration Other Than Kubernetes:

Other orchestration systems are available for particular purposes, even if Kubernetes is the most widely used:

- **Mesos Apache:** Mesos provides flexibility in managing large-scale applications and is frequently utilized in hybrid contexts.

- **Docker Swarm:** A more straightforward orchestration solution that is native to Docker, Docker Swarm is ideal for organizations with less complex orchestration requirements or smaller deployments.

3.3 Workflow management and automation

Because automation reduces human interaction and guarantees workflow repeatability, it is essential for expanding machine learning activities. Teams may design, oversee, and manage machine learning procedures with the help of workflow management solutions, guaranteeing the effectiveness, uniformity, and caliber of ML implementation.

Continuous Deployment and Integration (CI/CD) for Machine Learning:

Models may be frequently tested, validated, and deployed without requiring a lot of manual input thanks to CI/CD processes, which are widely used in software engineering and are essential to ML workflows in industrial contexts. For ML, CI/CD includes:

- In order to make sure that modifications to data, code, or configurations do not impair model performance, CI/CD pipelines automatically test models at each stage.

- Constant Integration of New Code and Data: CI pipelines cause updates to model training when new data becomes available, allowing models to adjust in real-time to changes.

- **Continuous Model Update Deployment:** The newest, most accurate models are always in use because of CD's automatic deployment of new models to production.

Data science teams can automate processes like data intake, training, and evaluation by using workflow management technologies like Apache Airflow, Kubeflow, and Luigi, which orchestrate intricate machine learning workflows. Important advantages include:

- **Task Automation:** Workflow managers free up time for model experimentation and fine-tuning by automating repetitive processes (such as training jobs and data preprocessing).

- **Dependency Management:** By enabling teams to specify task dependencies, workflow solutions guarantee that tasks are completed in a systematic, logical manner and without the need for manual intervention.

- **Scheduling and Monitoring:** While Kubeflow connects with Kubernetes to manage ML workflows, including real-time monitoring and error management, Airflow and other tools provide scheduling features.

The following are examples of MLOps platforms that provide specific workflow automation for machine learning: TFX (TensorFlow Extended) and MLflow

- **TFX:** Offers pre-made parts to automate processes like feature engineering, data validation, and model analysis.

- **MLflow:** makes it simple to deploy and keep an eye on models in production by tracking machine learning experiments and automating model deployment.

Organizations may build a robust software infrastructure that supports the full ML lifecycle, from development to production, by utilizing cloud-based MLOps solutions, Docker containerization, Kubernetes orchestration, and automated workflow management. Data science teams can scale their machine learning operations, swiftly adjust to changing data, and optimize the impact of their models across industrial applications thanks to this platform.

CHAPTER 4

EDGE COMPUTING AND HARDWARE ACCELERATORS

The efficiency, scalability, and performance of industrial machine learning applications are significantly impacted by the hardware and computing architecture selection. GPUs, TPUs, and ASICs are examples of specialized hardware accelerators that have become indispensable as machine learning models become more complicated and require more data. Furthermore, the emergence of edge computing makes it possible to place machine learning models nearer to data sources, which lowers latency and permits real-time decision-making in settings that are remote or mobile. Building effective machine learning infrastructure that satisfies the various needs of industrial applications requires an understanding of the advantages and disadvantages of various computing techniques and technology.

4.1 ASICs, TPUs, and GPUs

The speed and effectiveness of training and deploying machine learning models has been transformed by hardware accelerators. Three primary accelerator types Graphics Processing Units (GPUs), Tensor Processing Units (TPUs), and Application-Specific Integrated Circuits (ASICs) are at the heart of this transformation. Each of these accelerators has special advantages and is built to maximize particular kinds of machine learning workloads.

GPUs: Graphics Processing Units

GPUs were first created for graphic rendering, but their hundreds of cores provide tremendous parallelism, which makes them ideal for machine learning applications, particularly deep learning. Important traits consist of:

- **Parallel Processing Power:** GPUs are excellent at performing the large-scale data processing and matrix multiplication operations needed for deep learning.
- **Scalability:** Multi-GPU systems are supported by modern GPUs, such as NVIDIA's A100 or V100, and greatly accelerate training for very large models.

- **Versatility:** As general-purpose processors, GPUs can be utilized for a variety of machine learning applications, such as natural language processing and image recognition.

- **Popular Framework Support:** Because major machine learning frameworks like TensorFlow, PyTorch, and MXNet include libraries designed for GPU acceleration, researchers and industry practitioners prefer GPUs.

The following are Tensor Processing Units (TPUs):

Google created TPUs, which are specialized accelerators made to meet the demanding processing requirements of machine learning. Although TPUs were first developed to enhance Google's deep learning models, a broader audience can now access them thanks to their availability on Google Cloud. Among the main benefits are:

- **High Matrix Operations Efficiency:** Tensor-based calculations, which are essential to neural networks, are the focus of TPUs. TPUs are very effective for deep learning model training and inference because of their specialization.

- **Integrated Ecosystem of Software:** TensorFlow

and TPUs work well together, providing a smooth integration that makes model creation, training, and deployment easier.

- **Scalability Optimized:** For businesses working with intricate, large-scale machine learning models, cloud TPUs provide scalable solutions that can manage enormous workloads. Additionally, they come in various configurations, such as TPU v2 and TPU v3, each of which offers more processing capability for demanding machine learning workloads.

Application-specific integrated circuits, or ASICs, are as follows:

ASICs are specially made hardware components made for particular machine learning applications. They offer unmatched performance and efficiency for a given task. Despite being expensive to develop, they provide a number of benefits:

- **Customization for Specific ML Models:** By optimizing ASICs for particular workloads or algorithms, computational overhead and power consumption can be decreased.

- ASICs are perfect for applications where energy efficiency is crucial, including in mobile and Internet of Things devices, because they use less power than general-purpose processors.

- **Lower Latency and High Throughput:** ASICs' purpose-built design enables them to achieve lower latency and higher throughput, which speeds up processing in real-time applications.

The computational complexity of the model, financial limitations, and energy efficiency specifications are some of the variables that affect the choice of hardware accelerator for machine learning applications. Making wise choices in industrial machine learning requires a comprehensive grasp of each accelerator type's advantages and disadvantages.

4.2 ML's Edge Computing

Instead of depending entirely on centralized cloud or data center processing, edge computing processes data closer to the source. Because it allows for real-time data processing, lowers latency, and minimizes data transport costs, this method is becoming more and more common in industrial machine learning. Businesses can obtain more responsive and effective machine learning applications by installing models on edge devices, such as sensors, cameras, and Internet of Things devices. This is especially useful in settings with spotty or limited connectivity.

Edge Computing Applications in Machine Learning:
By facilitating real-time insights and decision-making at the network's edge, edge computing is revolutionizing a number of industries. Among the notable applications are:

- In factories, edge-based machine learning models evaluate camera and sensor data to identify flaws, streamline operations, and anticipate equipment failures in real time.

- **Healthcare and Medical gadgets:** Wearable health gadgets, such heart rate monitors and fall detectors, use edge computing to track patient vitals and deliver real-time feedback or alerts.

- **Autonomous Vehicles:** Autonomous vehicles analyze information from a wide range of sensors, such as lidar, radar, and cameras. Without depending on distant data centers, edge computing enables snap decisions.

- **Smart Cities and Retail:** Edge-enabled machine learning models facilitate a range of applications, including foot traffic analysis, facial recognition, and customized consumer interactions, which improve public safety and the retail experience.

Advantages of ML Model Deployment at the Edge: Compared to centralized processing, edge computing has the following advantages:

- **Decreased Latency:** Edge computing allows for quick reaction times by processing data locally, which is crucial for applications that require quick responses.

- **Data Security and Privacy:** By reducing the need to transport sensitive data to the cloud, edge processing improves privacy and helps comply with regulations.

- **Bandwidth Efficiency:** By sending only essential data or insights back to the cloud (instead of raw data), bandwidth is saved, which lowers expenses and network congestion.

Difficulties and Things to Think About for Edge ML:

Using ML at the edge has drawbacks despite its advantages:

- **Hardware Constraints:** Because edge devices frequently have low amounts of memory and processing power, compression methods or lightweight models are needed.

- Preserving energy efficiency is crucial, particularly for mobile or battery-operated edge devices.

- **Model Management and Updating**: It can be difficult to keep models updated at the edge, especially when there are many devices spread throughout far-flung areas. For effective management, over-the-air (OTA) update capabilities are essential.

Industrial machine learning applications that require speed, privacy, and local autonomy are made possible by edge computing. Leveraging the full potential of edge-based ML systems requires striking a balance between the computing demands of machine learning and the limitations of edge devices.

4.3 Choosing Hardware While Keeping Cost and Performance in Check

Budgetary restrictions and the performance needs of ML models must be balanced during the industrial machine learning hardware selection process. Deploying affordable yet effective solutions requires striking this balance, particularly as ML applications grow and demand more complex infrastructure.

Aspects to Take Into Account While Choosing ML Hardware:

A number of technical and budgetary considerations influence the selection of hardware for machine learning applications, including:

- **Model Complexity and Computational Demand:** Deep neural networks and other large, complicated models demand more potent technology, frequently requiring GPUs, TPUs, or ASICs. CPUs or less specialized technology can be adequate for simpler versions.

- **Budget and Cost Constraints:** TPUs and ASICs

are examples of high-performance hardware that can be expensive. Compromise may be required due to budgetary restrictions, particularly in non-critical applications.

- **Latency Requirements:** Real-time applications, such as industrial robotics or driverless cars, need technology with low latency that can make quick deductions. High-performance GPUs or edge-compatible ASICs might be required in certain situations.

- **Scalability Requirements:** Examine the hardware's ability to grow as data or model complexity increases. On-premises gear might have a set capacity, whereas cloud-based solutions might allow for more scalability.

- **Energy Efficiency and Sustainability:** In order to reduce energy costs in big deployments or for battery-powered devices, power-efficient hardware, such ASICs, is crucial. This aligns with corporate sustainability goals.

Cost-Effective Strategies for Optimizing ML Performance: Using a combination of hardware and software strategies, performance and cost may frequently be balanced:

- **Hybrid Cloud-Edge Architectures:** By utilizing cloud resources for more extensive training, businesses can balance cost and performance while maintaining some processing jobs on-premises or on edge devices.

- **Hardware Acceleration Only for Intensive operations**: To keep costs down, hardware accelerators such as GPUs and TPUs can be reserved for essential machine learning operations (such model training), leaving CPUs to do less demanding work.

- **Using Spot Instances and Reserved Instances on Cloud Platforms:** By utilizing discounted prices for computing resources, spot or reserved instances can lower expenses for cloud-based machine learning.

- **Model Optimization Techniques:** Methods such as distillation, pruning, and model quantization lower the computational requirements of machine learning models, enabling deployment on less costly hardware without sacrificing accuracy.

For industrial machine learning systems to be high-performance, scalable, and sustainable, hardware selection must strike a balance between cost and performance. Through the smart use of accelerators, edge computing, and cost-cutting strategies, businesses can successfully use machine learning solutions in a variety of industrial settings.

CHAPTER 5

INDUSTRIAL ML DATA MANAGEMENT AND SCALING

Effective machine learning (ML) in industrial contexts is predicated on scalable and well-managed data infrastructure. Large, high-quality datasets that can be processed and analyzed at scale are necessary for industrial machine learning applications in order to provide insights, increase decision-making, and improve forecasts. Organizations must have strong storage, processing, versioning, governance, and security procedures as data volume and complexity rise. This chapter explores the best practices for managing big data in machine learning, including crucial subjects related to processing, storage, governance, and compliance.

5.1 Processing and Storing Large Data

For industrial machine learning applications, the capacity to efficiently store and handle large datasets is critical.

Strong storage options and effective processing frameworks are necessary for managing massive volumes of data, from high-resolution sensor data in manufacturing to comprehensive transactional data in banking. Large-scale data ingestion, organization, and analysis are made possible by big data processing and storage, which supports the machine learning models that drive industrial applications.

Industrial ML Data Storage Solutions:

The type and volume of data, the frequency of access, and the need for scalability all play a role in choosing the best data storage option. Important storage options consist of:

- Structured, semi-structured, and unstructured data can all be stored in a single location thanks to data lakes. ML models may access a variety of data sources thanks to these systems' effective large-scale raw data storage. Data lakes frequently use technologies like Hadoop Distributed File System (HDFS), Azure Data Lake, and Amazon S3.

- **Data Warehouses:** Data warehouses facilitate sophisticated analytical processing and are optimized for relational, structured data. High-speed querying features offered by products like Google BigQuery, Amazon Redshift, and Snowflake make them appropriate for machine learning use cases requiring organized, queryable data.

- **NoSQL Databases:** With their great scalability and flexibility, NoSQL databases like MongoDB, Cassandra, and Redis are perfect for handling unstructured or semi-structured data. Applications that need low-latency data access, such as real-time suggestions, benefit greatly from NoSQL databases.

- **Hybrid and Multi-Cloud Storage**: Hybrid storage designs let businesses use the cloud's scalability for some datasets while keeping important data on-site. By avoiding vendor lock-in, multi-cloud systems also enable businesses to choose the best storage options available.

Data Processing Frameworks: Specialized frameworks that facilitate parallel processing, data translation, and large-scale analysis are necessary for processing massive datasets. Among the notable frameworks are:

- **Apache Spark:** Because Spark has in-memory compute features that speed up data processing operations, it is commonly used for distributed data processing. It works well with ML pipelines that need iterative processing and supports a variety of ML libraries.

- **Apache Flink:** Applications requiring real-time decision-making would benefit greatly from Flink, a stream processing framework that enables real-time processing of data as it is ingested.

- **Data Ingestion Pipelines and Kafka:** In order to process data as it flows from many sources, Kafka makes real-time data intake and streaming possible. Kafka, Spark, or Flink-built data ingestion pipelines guarantee that raw data is always accessible for machine learning training and inference.

In order to ensure effective and scalable processing, managing big data for machine learning necessitates a combination of technical best practices and strategic strategy.

- The technique of partitioning and indexing huge datasets improves processing efficiency by streamlining data access and cutting down on retrieval times.

- **Data Compression:** In dispersed contexts, compressing data speeds up data transport and lowers storage costs, but it's important to balance compression and processing time.

- **Caching Frequently Accessed Data:** By reducing latency during data processing, in-memory caches like Redis assist speed up access to frequently accessed data.

- **Cost Optimization Strategies:** Using managed data services or spot instances for big data processing activities can help reduce expenses without compromising performance.

5.2 Data Governance and Versioning

To preserve data integrity and guarantee that models are constructed and trained using dependable, consistent data, data governance and versioning are essential in industrial machine learning. Data versioning makes it possible to track changes to datasets, promoting openness and reproducibility in machine learning workflows, while data governance offers a framework for regulating data quality, access, and compliance.

The Value of Data Versioning in Machine Learning:

For the purpose of monitoring model performance over many data iterations and guaranteeing reproducibility, data versioning enables machine learning teams to document and oversee changes to datasets over time. Among the versioning techniques are:

- **Tracking Dataset Versions:** ML teams can track the precise data used in model training and evaluation by giving datasets distinct version identifiers, which makes analysis and debugging easier.

- Data lineage tracking is important for auditability and quality assurance since it guarantees that teams are aware of each dataset's origin, modifications, and history.

- **Implementing Version Control for Data Pipelines**: Data version control is made possible by tools such as Delta Lake and DVC (Data Version Control), which allow teams to handle datasets with the same level of precision as code and enhance data traceability.

The following are the principles and practices of data

governance: Data governance guarantees that data is correct, easily accessible, and complies with legal standards. Among the crucial elements of efficient data governance are:

- Consistency validation, duplication detection, and anomaly identification are examples of routine data quality checks that guarantee that only high-quality data is supplied into machine learning models.

- Data security and regulatory compliance are supported by minimizing the risk of illegal data access through the establishment of access restrictions based on user roles and responsibilities.

- **Metadata Management:** Data discovery and utilization in machine learning projects are facilitated by metadata, which includes details on data source, creation date, and ownership. This information enables teams to rapidly evaluate the quality and usefulness of datasets.

Data governance is facilitated by a number of tools and technologies, including:

- **Apache Atlas and Data Catalogs:** Tools such as Apache Atlas allow data discovery and lineage tracing by maintaining an extensive catalog of datasets and metadata.

- Platforms like Great Expectations enable teams to establish, verify, and track data quality standards, identifying possible problems before they affect machine learning models.

5.3 Security and Compliance

Data security and compliance are essential in industrial machine learning to safeguard confidential data and guarantee legal compliance. Maintaining secure data policies is crucial to avoiding legal and reputational issues as firms manage larger volumes of proprietary and personal data. Industry-specific compliance standards differ, and ML teams must modify their data handling procedures to satisfy these various demands.

Regulatory Compliance in Data Management: Data protection laws, which specify how businesses gather, handle, and preserve data, must be followed by industrial machine learning teams. Important regulatory frameworks consist of:

- **General Data Protection Regulation (GDPR):** GDPR requires enterprises that handle the data of EU citizens to adhere to stringent privacy and data protection standards, including rules on data collection, processing, and storage.
- The California Consumer Privacy Act (CCPA) protects Californians' right to privacy by allowing them to view, remove, and limit the sale of their personal information.
- **Regulations Particular to the Industry:** Certain industries are subject to certain data regulations, such as PCI-DSS for financial data and HIPAA for healthcare data. Respecting these guidelines is necessary to keep people's trust and stay out of trouble.

The implementation of strong security policies that reduce the danger of unauthorized access, data breaches, and cyberattacks is necessary to protect data in industrial machine learning environments. Important security precautions consist of:

- Sensitive information is protected even in the event that it is intercepted or viewed by unauthorized individuals thanks to data encryption, which is used both in transit and at rest.

- Only authorized personnel are able to view or alter sensitive data thanks to the prevention of unauthorized access provided by role-based access controls (RBAC) and multi-factor authentication (MFA).

- **Data Masking and Anonymization:** Data masking or anonymization techniques can help safeguard privacy while maintaining the analytical usefulness of datasets that contain personal information.

- **Regular Audits and Penetration Testing**: Regular security audits and penetration testing ensure data protection stays current by identifying and addressing vulnerabilities in data systems.

Technologies & Tools for Security and Compliance:
Organizations can use a number of tools to help data management security and compliance, including:

- **Data Loss Prevention (DLP) Solutions:** DLP products enable adherence to privacy requirements by preventing sensitive data from being accessed or transferred inappropriately.

- Platforms for Compliance Management: Tools for managing compliance workflows are available on platforms such as Collibra, which guarantee that data handling procedures adhere to legal regulations.

- **Security Information and Event Management (SIEM) Systems:** SIEM systems assist firms detect and lessen any threats by offering real-time monitoring and alerting of security events.

For industrial machine learning, it is essential to implement strong compliance and security procedures in data management. These procedures protect private data, guarantee adherence to the law, and strengthen confidence in machine learning systems. Organizations build a strong basis for machine learning (ML) that complies with industry standards and legal frameworks by implementing safe, legal, and scalable data management procedures.

CHAPTER 6

MODEL TRAINING AND TUNING AUTOMATION

Automation in model training and tuning is essential as machine learning (ML) systems grow in complexity and scale across several domains. By quickly iterating on setups and testing variants, automated procedures improve model performance, guarantee effective resource allocation, and expedite repetitive activities. With an emphasis on Automated Machine Learning (AutoML), hyperparameter optimization, and the sophisticated methods of meta-learning and transfer learning, this chapter discusses important facets of automation in model training. By improving ML pipelines, each of these strategies seeks to help data scientists and ML engineers create, fine-tune, and implement reliable models more quickly and effectively.

6.1 Machine Learning Automated (AutoML)

By automating procedures like feature engineering, model selection, and hyperparameter tuning, Automated Machine Learning (AutoML) streamlines the machine learning workflow. AutoML enables non-experts to understand machine learning (ML) and relieves proficient ML practitioners of time-consuming activities so they may concentrate on more complex decisions.

Model Training and Selection

Selecting the best model for a task in typical machine learning workflows requires trial and error using a variety of algorithms, each of which takes a substantial amount of tweaking and training time. This is addressed by autoML systems, such as Google AutoML, H2O.ai, and DataRobot, which automatically rank various models according to performance metrics. Usually, this procedure consists of:

- **Algorithm Selection:** AutoML eliminates the need to manually test every possibility by identifying the most promising algorithms for a dataset.

- **Methods of Assembly:** AutoML frequently creates ensembles from several models, utilizing the advantages of several techniques to improve performance.

- **Performance metrics and scoring are as follows:** Using predetermined measures (such as accuracy, F1 score, or AUC), AutoML evaluates models and chooses the best-performing models for additional analysis.

Automation of Feature Engineering

Model success depends on feature engineering, which is the process of developing and choosing pertinent features from unprocessed data. AutoML technologies automate this process using a range of methods, producing strong feature sets that enhance model performance without necessitating domain knowledge. Among the methods are:

- **Transformation of Numerical and Categorical Data:** All data formats are compatible with machine learning models thanks to automated normalization, scaling, and encoding of categorical variables.

- **Interaction Generation:** AutoML can capture intricate relationships in the data by generating feature interactions that human feature engineering could overlook.

- **Dimensionality Reduction:** To prevent overfitting and lower computational cost, AutoML makes use of dimensionality reduction techniques (such as PCA or feature selection).

Tuning Hyperparameters

One of the most time-consuming parts of machine learning is frequently hyperparameter tuning. By iterating through a variety of hyperparameters to get the best settings for every model, AutoML automates this process. AutoML platforms frequently incorporate methods like grid search, random search, and Bayesian optimization to find high-performing configurations with little assistance from humans.

The advantages and difficulties of autoML

- By enabling a wider variety of users to access intricate model-building operations, AutoML democratizes machine learning. Although it speeds up model construction and increases ML teams' productivity, it has certain drawbacks.
- **Interpretability Issues:** Highly automated models might not be transparent, which makes it difficult to decipher the underlying mechanics or troubleshoot surprising outcomes.
- **Data Quality Dependency:** AutoML systems are

highly dependent on the quantity and quality of data; regardless of automation, low-quality data might result in less-than-ideal models.

- **Resource Intensity:** AutoML procedures, particularly model selection and hyperparameter tuning, can be computationally costly and require a large amount of cloud resources.

6.2 Techniques for Hyperparameter Optimization

Model performance is greatly influenced by hyperparameters, which are settings that control how ML algorithms behave. The optimal configuration is found with the least amount of computational overhead using effective hyperparameter optimization (HPO). By eliminating the need for manual tuning, automated HPO procedures maximize efficiency and speed up model training.

Grid Search

One of the simplest yet most used HPO strategies is grid search. It entails establishing a collection of hyperparameters and thoroughly looking through every potential combination. Grid search makes sure that every parameter combination is examined, despite the fact that it is computationally demanding. This method works well in search areas that are smaller and have fewer alternative configurations.

Random Search

For huge search spaces, random search is a more effective method than grid search since it chooses hyperparameter combinations at random. According to studies, random search frequently outperforms grid search with fewer trials because it does not explore every possible combination in-depth. When performance is considerably influenced by only a selection of hyperparameters, random search is especially helpful.

The Bayesian optimization technique

A probabilistic method for HPO, Bayesian optimization strikes a compromise between exploitation (improving on existing settings) and exploration (trying new hyperparameter settings). By building a surrogate model to forecast performance based on previous trials, tools such as Optuna and Spearmint apply Bayesian optimization.

Bayesian optimization is perfect for complex models with vast hyperparameter spaces since it can efficiently identify optimal settings with fewer trials.

Algorithms that evolve

Natural selection serves as the inspiration for evolutionary algorithms, which evolve a population of candidate configurations across many generations in order to maximize hyperparameters. By iteratively refining hyperparameter settings based on fitness scores, techniques like genetic algorithms use operations like mutation and crossover. Deep neural networks and other sophisticated models with large parameter spaces can benefit greatly from evolutionary approaches.

Optimization Based on Gradients

Hypergradient Descent and other gradient-based HPOs use the hyperparameter gradients to fine-tune them in the direction of improvement. Although computationally efficient, this method is usually restricted to differentiable parameters. Although it is less prevalent in traditional machine learning, it exhibits potential in deep learning applications where it is possible to optimize parameters continuously.

HPO Frameworks and Tools

To make the application of these strategies easier, a number of HPO frameworks have been developed, such as:

1. **Hyperopt:** Supports both basic and complex search spaces and provides Bayesian optimization.

2. **Optuna:** A versatile, quick optimization library with sophisticated visualization and trimming features.

3. **Ray Tune:** Suitable for large-scale machine learning projects, this distributed hyperparameter tuning tool supports numerous optimization strategies.

Effective hyperparameter tuning can decrease computing costs, enhance performance, and significantly cut down on model training times. When integrated into machine learning workflows, automated HPO guarantees that models continuously produce the best outcomes with the least amount of human involvement.

6.3 Transfer Learning and Meta-Learning

Advanced machine learning approaches like meta-learning

and transfer learning use past information to speed up model training and enhance performance on novel challenges. In industrial machine learning, where reusing pre-existing models can save time, money, and processing power, both approaches are essential.

Learning to Learn (Meta-Learning)

Teaching models to swiftly adjust to new tasks with less data is the main goal of meta-learning. Meta-learning algorithms learn to recognize patterns and insights from past tasks rather than training models from scratch, which facilitates generalization to new situations. Important strategies for meta-learning consist of:

- **MAML, or model-agnostic meta-learning:** To create a flexible model that can learn new tasks with little data, MAML trains models on a range of tasks.

- **Both one-shot and few-shot learning:** By training on similar tasks, few-shot learning allows models to learn from a small number of samples. This is especially helpful in situations where there is a shortage of data.

- **Metric-Based Learning:** Metric-based meta-learning models use fewer training samples to facilitate classification or clustering by learning to quantify similarity between data points.

Applications like recommendation systems, e-commerce personalization, and anomaly detection that demand quick model deployment, personalization, or adaptability frequently employ meta-learning approaches.

Transfer Learning

Transfer learning eliminates the need for large amounts of training data by using the information a pre-trained model has gained on one task to enhance performance on a related one. Typical methods include of:

- **Optimizing Pre-Trained Models:** By retraining the last layers of a previously trained model on a different task, fine-tuning enables the model to maintain its general characteristics while adjusting to task-specific patterns. This method is frequently applied in natural language processing (e.g., sentiment analysis) and computer vision (e.g., picture classification).

- **Extraction of Features:** This method involves extracting the intermediate representations (also known as "features") of a pre-trained model and using them as input to another model. By giving the model a solid foundation without requiring it to be retrained from beginning, feature extraction speeds up training.

- **Adaptation of Domain:** Effective transfer is made possible by domain adaptation techniques, which help align the features from both domains when the source and target tasks have different data distributions.

Benefits and Use Cases of Industrial Machine Learning

In industrial machine learning applications where it is not feasible to build a model from scratch, meta-learning and transfer learning are advantageous. For example:

- The following are personalized recommendations: Transfer learning eliminates the requirement for intensive data collection by customizing general recommendation models to the preferences of specific users.
- The use of predictive maintenance By using knowledge from similar equipment, meta-learning models can adjust to new gear or sensors in

industrial settings, enabling precise equipment failure predictions with little additional data.

- **Diagnostics and Healthcare:** In order to create medical imaging models that generalize across different scan types and situations and allow for quicker and more precise diagnostic predictions, transfer learning is frequently utilized.

Difficulties and Restrictions

Notwithstanding the benefits of transfer learning and meta-learning, there are certain issues to take into account:

- Performance may suffer if there are large data transfers, even though transfer learning relies on the source and target domains being sufficiently similar.

- **Requirements for computation:** Large pre-trained models can still require a significant amount of processing power to train, even though transfer learning lowers the amount of training data needed.

- **Transparency and Interpretability:** Since the features or knowledge that transfer learning models convey are frequently abstract representations from deep neural networks, they might be challenging to understand.

Organizations can overcome data limits, cut expenses, and shorten training times by utilizing meta-learning and transfer learning. These methods,

Together with automated model training and tweaking, they open the door to more flexible and agile machine learning solutions that can be tailored to a variety of applications and changing business requirements.

CHAPTER 7

MODEL UPDATING AND CONTINUOUS LEARNING

Models used in real-world industrial machine learning (ML) applications need to adjust to shifting user behaviors, data patterns, and environments. Maintaining the model's performance and relevance over time requires constant learning and updating. The concepts of continuous learning, strategies for managing model drift and retraining, and the crucial function of feedback loops in real-time model updates are all covered in detail in this chapter. These techniques guarantee that models not only produce accurate forecasts but also dynamically adjust to fresh data, changing needs, and emerging patterns.

7.1 Continuous Learning Concepts

The ability of a model to adjust as new data becomes available, enabling it to get better over time without needing to be completely restrained from start, is referred to as continuous learning, online learning, or incremental learning. In industrial settings, where data can change quickly and it's imperative that models remain in line with evolving realities, this method is very useful. Models are kept resilient and their performance isn't compromised in dynamic contexts because of continuous learning.

Primary Features of Continuous Learning

- **Incremental Data Integration:** Instead of waiting for recurring retraining cycles, continuous learning enables models to continuously integrate new data. Applications like fraud detection, where new patterns must be promptly identified to preserve security, or e-commerce recommendation systems, where customer preferences may change often, are particularly affected by this.

- **Reducing Downtime:** Continuous learning reduces operational disruptions by updating models without interrupting them, which is essential for applications in real-time monitoring systems, manufacturing, and finance.

- The cost-effectiveness of this Conventional retraining can be time-consuming and computationally costly. By enabling the model to change gradually without undergoing a total redesign, continuous learning lowers these expenses.

Industrial Applications of Continuous Learning

Adaptive, responsive machine learning models are beneficial in a wide range of industries, making continuous learning applicable:

- The use of predictive maintenance Machine sensors continuously collect new data in industrial environments. Using this data, a continuous learning model can forecast equipment failures or maintenance requirements, modifying its predictions as circumstances change.

- **Healthcare Monitoring:** In customized medicine, when patient data, such as test results or vital signs, changes over time, ongoing learning is beneficial. Continuous learning models can improve their predictions by incorporating fresh patient data, which aids in anticipating health hazards and suggesting prompt interventions.

- **Identifying Financial Fraud:** Since fraud trends change quickly, continual learning is very beneficial for fraud detection algorithms. Strong security is ensured by models that can keep up with new fraudulent activities by learning from fresh data in real time.

Models can remain relevant in rapidly evolving situations thanks to continuous learning, which fosters efficiency and adaptability. For industrial applications where reliable, real-time performance is crucial, this feature is indispensable.

7.2 Managing Retraining and Model Drift

When a model's performance deteriorates over time as a result of shifting data distributions or patterns, this is known as model drift. Changes in user behavior, seasonal influences, or modifications to the underlying data generation mechanisms are some of the causes of drift. An essential part of ongoing learning and model maintenance is identifying and correcting model drift.

Types of Model Drift

1. **Concept Drift:** Takes place when the connection

between target variables and input features shifts. For instance, in the retail industry, unforeseen changes in the market may cause the relationship between product sales and seasonality to alter, necessitating that the model modify its forecasts.

2. Changes in the distribution of input data that do not impact the underlying relationships are referred to as "data drift." The input data may vary in a manufacturing setting if sensor calibrations change, necessitating that the model re-learn the data properties in order to continue operating.

3. **Decay in Performance:** Performance decay occurs when the accuracy or dependability of the model deteriorates over time, frequently as a result of undiscovered drift. In high-stakes applications like financial forecasts or medical diagnostics, this is especially worrisome.

Drift Detection Mechanisms:

- **Methods for Identifying and Resolving Drift:** Data distributions can be tracked over time using tools such as the Population Stability Index (PSI), the Kolmogorov-Smirnov (KS) test, and statistical process control methods. These methods can identify variations that point to drift by comparing the distributions of the data today with those from the past.

- **Consistent Model Retraining**: Although it requires a lot of resources, scheduled retraining periods can help reduce drift. When drift is predictable, like with seasonal variations, this strategy works well.

- **Retraining Dynamically using Triggered Events**: Certain systems employ drift detection triggers to start retraining only when drift is detected, as opposed to retraining at predetermined intervals. By eliminating needless retraining and allocating resources only when drift has a substantial effect on performance, this method lowers computing overhead.

- **Adaptive Rates of Learning:** The model can react more rapidly to recent data without overfitting to noise in some continuous learning systems by varying the learning rate. This method is frequently applied in real-time applications and reinforcement learning.

Industrial Examples of Model Drift and Retraining

- **Financial Markets:** Models used in algorithmic trading have to adjust to the erratic market conditions. Because market fluctuations, regulatory changes, and economic upheavals frequently cause model drift, frequent retraining is crucial for precise forecasting.

- **Optimizing the Supply Chain:** Variations in demand trends might lead to predictive model drift in logistics. Models can be retrained to improve supply chain flow and inventory management by identifying these changes.

- **Weather and Climate Forecast:** Long-term environmental changes must be taken into consideration by models used in climate analysis and weather prediction. Predictions are kept accurate and relevant by retraining models using fresh atmospheric and environmental data.

Maintaining consistent model performance requires managing model drift, particularly in applications where it may lead to expensive mistakes or safety hazards. By putting strong drift detection and retraining techniques into practice, performance deterioration is reduced and models are kept reliable over time.

7.3 Real-Time Update Feedback Loops

Feedback loops are essential to model updating because they continuously improve models by integrating user feedback, performance data, and fresh ideas. Real-time feedback loops work especially well in settings where quick corrections are required to preserve accuracy and peak performance.

The following are some examples of feedback loop types:

- **Human-in-the-Loop (HITL) Feedback:** Human experts evaluate and revise model predictions in HITL systems, then feed the updated predictions back into the model to enhance learning. This method is frequently used in applications where precision is crucial, such medical diagnostics, where expert confirmation is required prior to modifying model outputs.

- **Autonomous Feedback Loops:** In order to improve accuracy, automated feedback systems gather data on model performance in real time and incorporate it back into the model. This is common in autonomous systems that constantly use sensor data to improve their decision-making algorithms, like self-driving automobiles.

- **Feedback on Consumer Behavior:** Feedback from user activities (clicks, purchases, likes) is collected and used to instantly recalibrate the model in systems that offer personalized suggestions or customer interaction. This guarantees that the model will provide a personalized experience by adjusting to user preferences as they change.

Model updating through the implementation of feedback loops

- **Real-Time Data Integration:** By collecting data on how models function in actual environments, feedback loops enable models to be updated with new information as it becomes available. For instance, in e-commerce, product recommendation algorithms can be informed by user engagement data (such search searches or past purchases) to make sure they remain relevant.

- **Feedback from A/B testing and validation:** One way to provide feedback for ongoing model improvement is through A/B testing. ML engineers can collect real-time performance data by comparing various iterations of a model, which helps them guide updates that prioritize the model that performs the best.

- **Constant Quality Inspections:** When a model's performance deviates from expected norms, feedback loops might incorporate quality checks, such accuracy or error rate monitoring, into the machine learning process. This increases model reliability by ensuring that aberrant or low-quality predictions are identified and fixed.

Advantages of real-time feedback

- **Agility in Adaptive Systems:** Real-time feedback allows adaptive systems, like intelligent manufacturing robots, to react to shifting environmental conditions, improving operational efficiency and decreasing downtime. This is one of the advantages of real-time feedback in industrial applications.

- **Enhanced User Experience**: Constant feedback enables models to react dynamically to user interactions in customer-facing apps, guaranteeing a tailored and captivating experience.

- **Risk Reduction in High-Stakes Situations:** Feedback loops enable rapid modifications in applications that have important financial or safety ramifications. Feedback, for example, can reduce risk in financial trading algorithms by reacting quickly to changes in the market.

Difficulties with Feedback Loop Implementation

- **Latency Issues:** If feedback integration is not properly handled, it can cause latency, particularly in real-time applications. For real-time performance, it is crucial to make sure that feedback is quickly analyzed and integrated.

- **Recommendation Quality:** Not every feedback has the same value, and noisy or poor-quality input might make a model perform worse. For feedback to be useful, methods like data validation and filtering are crucial.

- **Risks to Privacy and Security:** Feedback loops in

user-facing programs have the potential to record private information. Protecting user privacy requires putting strong security measures in place and making sure that data protection laws are followed.

Real-time model updating relies heavily on feedback loops, which enable models to adjust to changing environmental conditions and new data. When feedback mechanisms are implemented well, models remain relevant and responsive, improving performance and guaranteeing dependability in changing industrial environments.

ML models may continue to be precise, effective, and responsive in dynamic industrial settings thanks to feedback loops, ongoing learning, and model retraining. These methods are essential in fields where static models are unable to satisfy changing operational needs or data demands. Organizations may maintain resilient and flexible machine learning systems that deliver consistent value and dependability across a range of applications by utilizing real-time feedback, managing model drift, and implementing continuous learning.

CHAPTER 8

INTEGRATION OF MLOPS AND DEVOPS

A significant advancement in the deployment, monitoring, and administration of machine learning models is the combination of DevOps with Machine Learning Operations (MLOps). Applying DevOps concepts to machine learning (ML) procedures can improve productivity, optimize workflows, and guarantee reliable performance in production settings as ML and software engineering become more intertwined. The application of DevOps principles to the ML lifecycle, tools and methods for monitoring and debugging ML models in production, and strategies for creating reliable version control for both models and data are all covered in this chapter. Teams can handle ML systems with accuracy, scalability, and resilience thanks to these tactics.

8.1 Machine Learning Principles of DevOps

In software development, DevOps places a strong emphasis on teamwork, automation, and continuous delivery—all of which are in line with the requirements of machine learning operations. However, these ideas must be modified to meet the particular needs of ML workflows in order to integrate DevOps into ML processes, or MLOps. MLOps assists in managing the complete ML lifecycle with the same level of rigor as traditional software engineering, from data management and model deployment to ongoing training and performance monitoring.

MLOps Using Core DevOps Principles

- **Continuous Integration (CI):** CI in the context of machine learning entails regularly incorporating code modifications into the ML pipeline. This may entail improving model architectures, adding new features, and upgrading data preprocessing programs. Every component undergoes automated testing to guarantee seamless integration with other ML pipeline components, reducing errors and increasing efficiency.

- CD stands for Continuous Deployment. CD in MLOps refers to the frequent or event-driven deployment of updated models into production environments (e.g., when model performance data suggest a need for retraining). Automated deployment keeps production performance high, guarantees smooth upgrades, and reduces downtime.

- **IaC, or Infrastructure as Code:** With IaC, ML engineers may use code to specify, provision, and manage infrastructure (including networks, storage, and processing power). This facilitates consistency throughout several deployment stages, from development to production, and makes it simpler to track infrastructure changes and replicate setups.

- **Automated Validation and Testing:** In MLOps, automated testing encompasses not only integration and unit tests but also specific tests for model performance and data validation. This guarantees feature compatibility, data quality, and the maintenance of model correctness in various settings. In order to avoid data or model drift, which can result in decreased production performance, automated testing is essential.

Advantages of Using DevOps Principles in ML

- **Enhanced Efficiency:** Teams can concentrate on innovation and model optimization by automating tedious processes like data preparation, model training, and deployment.

- MLOps practices guarantee that teams can scale models and processes without creating bottlenecks as ML systems get more complicated.

- A more integrated ML lifecycle results from the adoption of DevOps, which promotes a collaborative atmosphere among data scientists, ML developers, and IT teams.

- In machine learning (ML), where models require constant retraining and updating to stay effective, DevOps' emphasis on a quick development and release cycle is especially beneficial.

Organizations may preserve consistency, dependability, and scalability in their ML systems and guarantee that models continue to function effectively in production settings by coordinating ML workflows with DevOps principles.

8.2 Tracking and Troubleshooting Machine Learning Models in Production

To make sure a model produces accurate and trustworthy predictions when it is put into production, performance monitoring and prompt problem-solving are crucial. ML models necessitate specific monitoring for data, predictions, and model behavior, in contrast to traditional software, where monitoring concentrates on system metrics. Debugging tools assist MLOps by assisting in the real-time identification and correction of problems.

Primary Domains of ML Model Surveillance

- **Data Quality Surveillance:** Model accuracy may be impacted by modifications to the data's properties, such as missing numbers or variations in distribution. Ensuring that the model receives consistent, high-quality data inputs requires monitoring the quality of the incoming data.

- **Accuracy of Prediction and Detection of Drift:** Assessing model accuracy and identifying drift is aided by comparing model predictions to actual results, or ground truth. When a model's performance departs from baseline measures, drift detection technologies can see it and send out notifications for recalibration or retraining.

- **Monitoring throughput and latency:** Monitoring the latency and throughput of model predictions is essential for real-time systems in order to guarantee prompt answers. Problems with latency could be a sign of model or underlying infrastructure performance constraints.

- **Model Utilization of Resources**: It is crucial to keep an eye on CPU, GPU, and memory utilization in order to assess the model's effectiveness and spot areas for improvement. Overuse of resources can be a sign that infrastructure needs to be scaled or the model needs to be improved.

Tools for Tracking and Troubleshooting Machine Learning Models

- **Prometheus and Grafana**: Model performance metrics can be tracked using these widely used tools for tracking and displaying system data. They make it possible to visualize parameters like response time, resource usage, and custom model accuracy ratings in real time.

- **MLflow and TensorFlow Extended (TFX)**: End-to-end platforms for tracking and controlling the ML lifecycle are TFX and MLflow. They offer resources for maintaining versioned models in production, tracking data quality, and keeping an eye on performance.

- **Kubiflow and Seldon Core:** These tools provide specific capabilities for Kubernetes ML model serving and monitoring. They enable MLOps teams to sustain model performance at scale with integrated monitoring, alerting, and visualization features.

The following are some effective debugging techniques:

- **Error Analysis:** Analyzing inaccurate predictions to find trends or underlying problems in the data is a common step in debugging machine learning models. Biases or inaccuracies that may need modifying the model or data pretreatment pipeline can be found through error analysis.

- **Traceability Logging:** Engineers can track and replicate problems by meticulously recording data inputs, transformations, and forecasts, particularly when looking into errors or anomalies.

- **A/B Testing to Compare Models:** MLOps teams may assess and compare performance in real-world scenarios by conducting A/B testing with several model versions in production. This is helpful for verifying model updates prior to their complete implementation.

ML models operate dependably in production thanks to monitoring and debugging. Organizations may maximize the return on their machine learning investments, preserve model accuracy, and detect problems early by combining these tools and approaches.

8.3 Data and Model Version Control

Because version control guarantees consistency, reproducibility, and traceability, it is crucial for managing models and datasets in MLOps. ML version control must take into consideration datasets, feature engineering scripts, and model parameters, all of which might affect model performance, in contrast to traditional version control, which just considers code.

Difficulties with ML Version Control

- **Data Versioning:** Data, in contrast to code, can be enormous and ever-changing. To guarantee reproducible model training and testing, versioning data necessitates tracking several datasets and metadata.

- **Versioning the Model:** Every training cycle or hyperparameter change causes models to change, hence robust versioning is necessary to efficiently manage several model iterations. Monitoring model designs, hyperparameters, and outcomes facilitates debugging and helps to preserve consistency.

- **Environment Consistency:** To guarantee that models can be deployed between phases without encountering compatibility problems, ML environments, including libraries, dependencies, and infrastructure, need to be versioned. This is particularly important for intricate pipelines since inconsistencies can arise from even small changes in dependency.

Best practices in version control

- The use of specialized ML version control tools is one of the best practices in version control for machine learning. Data, model, and environment versions can be managed with the use of tools like Pachyderm and DVC (Data Version Control). By extending version control to non-code materials through integration with Git, these solutions facilitate the tracking of changes throughout the ML pipeline.

- **Creating Versioning Guidelines:** Clarity and consistency are preserved by creating standards for identifying and classifying data, model, and configuration versions. Clear descriptions and metadata are essential for versioning in order to track changes and comprehend dependencies.

- **Metadata Tracking for Contextual Information:** Monitoring metadata like the model training date, dataset source, and important parameters is part of an efficient version control system. This data gives each model version context, allowing for speedy rollbacks when necessary.

Strong version control has the following advantages:

- **Reproducibility:** Teams can exactly duplicate experiments thanks to version control, which guarantees that models can be re-trained and validated using the same datasets and parameters. In industries including healthcare, banking, and research, this is essential for maintaining scientific integrity and regulatory compliance.

- **Traceability and Collaboration:** Every step of the ML pipeline should be versioned so that team members can quickly exchange updates, roll back changes, and troubleshoot problems. This is particularly helpful in large teams where several stakeholders work together on various pipeline components.

- **Model Audits and Compliance Made Simpler**: Version control offers a clear audit record of the training, validation, and deployment of models for companies subject to regulations. This traceability expedites the paperwork process and helps meet regulatory standards.

The following are examples of version control tools in

use:

- **Git and Git-LFS (Large File Storage):** Git-LFS is especially helpful for handling big datasets that surpass Git's storage constraints, whereas Git is commonly used for code versioning. These tools facilitate reproducibility in the machine learning workflow by enabling smooth version management for both code and data.

- **Data Version Control, or DVC:** To keep track of model files and dataset versions, DVC interfaces with Git. DVC makes model iteration and collaboration easier by versioning big datasets and machine learning workflows.

- **Registries for Models:** It is simple to roll back to earlier versions or deploy updated versions with no risk thanks to tools like MLflow and TensorFlow Model Registry, which maintain several model versions along with information.

For ML projects to remain transparent, reproducible, and intact, version control for both data and models is essential. Data and model lifecycles can be safely managed by MLOps teams by utilizing specialized tools and adhering to best practices.

making certain that every phase of the machine learning process is optimized for reliable performance and traceability.

CHAPTER 9

ETHICAL AND REGULATORY CONSIDERATIONS

Ethical and legal issues have become more prominent in conversations among practitioners, companies, and legislators as machine learning (ML) technology becomes more and more integrated into a variety of industrial applications. Gaining public trust, adhering to legal requirements, and promoting innovation all depend on ML systems functioning in a fair, responsible, and sustainable manner. This chapter explores three important topics: the environmental impact of industrial machine learning, data privacy and regulatory compliance, and bias and fairness in ML applications. Organizations may create strong machine learning systems that are not only efficient but also morally and responsibly sound by taking these factors into account.

9.1 Fairness and Bias in Industrial Machine Learning Applications

Machine learning bias has the potential to produce discriminatory results in a number of industries, such as employment, lending, healthcare, and law enforcement, by treating people and groups unfairly. ML systems may unintentionally reinforce preexisting biases or introduce new ones since they frequently learn from historical data. Therefore, to guarantee fairness in ML applications, bias must be recognized and mitigated.

Comprehending Bias in Machine Learning
Types of Bias:

- Historical data that exhibits social prejudices, such as the underrepresentation of minority groups or distorted results depending on socioeconomic position, gender, or ethnicity, is known as data bias.

- Data biases may be exacerbated by algorithmic bias, which happens when algorithms inherently favor particular results due to their design or training.

- Inaccuracies in data collection techniques can lead to measurement bias, which can skew the representation of the phenomena being measured.

- The ramifications of bias are as follows: Unfair decisions, a decline in public trust, and legal repercussions for businesses are all possible outcomes of biased machine learning algorithms. Thus, the first step in mitigating bias is to identify its sources.

Detecting Bias in ML Systems

- **Data Audits:** Evaluate training datasets in-depth to determine their representativeness and spot any biases. This entails examining the data's demographic distribution and how it relates to results.

- **Bias Detection Tools:** To systematically check models for bias, use frameworks and tools like AI Fairness 360, Fairlearn, and What-If Tool. These tools can assist in identifying gaps and visualizing model predictions across various demographic groupings.

- **Stakeholder Engagement:** Include a range of stakeholders in the development process to offer viewpoints and insights that may reveal prejudices the development team has missed.

Mitigating Bias in ML Applications

- **Data Preprocessing Techniques:** Before training models, use strategies like adversarial debiasing, data augmentation, and re-sampling to produce balanced datasets that reduce bias.

- Employ algorithmic fairness techniques that specifically seek to lessen bias, such as divergent effect analysis, equalized odds, and demographic parity. These methods guarantee that no group is favored in model predictions.

- **Continuous Monitoring and Adjustment**: Provide systems for ongoing evaluation of model performance and production equity. To counteract new biases, change models and datasets often in response to feedback and new data.

Promoting an Equitable Culture

Encourage ML practitioners and stakeholders to receive training and education on bias and fairness. More ethical development processes and more equitable results can result from fostering a culture that values ethical considerations in machine learning.

Organizations can guarantee that their machine learning

systems are equitable and responsible by proactively detecting and resolving bias. This will increase public trust and lower the possibility of regulatory scrutiny.

9.2 Compliance and Data Privacy

Organizations operating in different jurisdictions must navigate data privacy rules and ensure compliance because machine learning algorithms frequently rely on enormous volumes of personal data. The significance of safeguarding people's data rights and privacy has been emphasized by the introduction of laws like the General Data Protection Regulation (GDPR) in the European Union.

Key Principles of Data Privacy Regulations

- **Transparency:** Organizations must be open and honest about the ways in which they gather, handle, and use personal data. This involves being transparent with people about their rights and the intended use of their data.

- **Consent:** Prior to processing personal data, informed consent must be obtained. Companies need to make sure people know they can revoke their consent at any moment.

- **Data Minimization:** Only gather the information required for particular uses. Reducing the amount of data collected lowers privacy risks and is consistent with the idea of limiting exposure to possible security breaches.

- **Right to Access and Deletion**: People are entitled to see their personal information and ask that it be removed. For organizations to effectively handle these demands, procedures must be in place.

Managing Data Privacy Laws

- **GDPR Compliance:** Companies that operate in the EU or target EU citizens are required to abide by GDPR. This entails designating a Data Protection Officer (DPO), implementing data protection by default and by design, and keeping track of processing activity.

- **CCPA Adherence:** Similar safeguards are offered by the California Consumer Privacy Act (CCPA) in the US. Organizations are required to provide opt-out choices and disclose their data gathering practices to Californians.

- **Transferring data internationally:** Organizations must make sure that international regulations are followed when moving personal data across borders. Legal data transfers can be facilitated by putting in place binding business regulations or Standard Contractual Clauses (SCCs).

Implementing privacy by design in machine learning workflows

- **Data Anonymization and Pseudonymization:** Using methods to anonymize or pseudonymous personal data improves privacy protections and lowers the risk of data breaches.

- **Frameworks for Data Governance:** Organizations can ensure compliance with privacy rules by defining data ownership, access controls, and accountability mechanisms with the aid of a strong data governance structure.

Affect on ML Model Development

- **Data Lifecycle Management:** Use data lifecycle management techniques to guarantee adherence to regulations at every stage of the data lifetime, from gathering and processing to deleting and retaining.

- **Ethical Considerations in Data Usage:** Review data usage procedures on a regular basis to make sure that personal data is handled ethically, especially when it comes to sensitive data categories (e.g., financial data, health data).

In an increasingly data-driven world, companies can safeguard people's rights, reduce legal risks, and foster stakeholder trust by putting data privacy and compliance first.

9.3 Industrial ML's Effect on the Environment

The environmental impact of industrial machine learning applications, especially with regard to energy usage and carbon emissions, has become a critical concern as these systems grow in size. Large models can demand a lot of processing power to train and implement in manufacturing, which raises energy consumption and increases carbon emissions.

Comprehending the Effect on the Environment

- **Energy Use in Machine Learning Training:** Deep learning model training frequently entails laborious computational operations requiring large energy inputs. According to research, throughout the course of their lifetimes, huge language models can release as much carbon as five automobiles.

- **The operations of the data center:** The environmental impact of data centers housing machine learning models is influenced by their energy usage. The overall effect is influenced by cooling systems, hardware efficiency, and energy sources (renewable versus non-renewable).

The following are some methods for lessening the impact on the environment:

- Energy-Efficient Algorithms: Energy consumption can be decreased by creating and implementing algorithms that use less processing power. Without appreciably compromising performance, methods like information distillation, quantization, and model pruning can assist in producing smaller, more effective models.

- **Utilizing Sustainable Energy Sources:** Businesses

that use sustainable energy sources, such solar or wind, can lessen their influence on the environment. A growing number of tech firms are pledging to use renewable energy to power their data centers.

- **Optimizing Infrastructure utilization:** Energy waste can be decreased by utilizing cloud computing systems that optimize resource utilization and provide dynamic scaling. This involves making use of resource-efficient serverless architectures and containerization technologies.

Carbon Footprint Measurement and Reporting

- **Carbon Footprint Evaluation:** The carbon footprint of an organization's machine learning processes should be evaluated and tracked. Energy use and emissions related to ML model deployment and training can be measured with the aid of tools and frameworks.

- **Reporting on Sustainability:** Accountability is promoted and greener behaviors are encouraged when environmental impact is reported transparently. Tracking progress can be facilitated by establishing sustainability-related key performance indicators (KPIs).

Encouraging Sustainable Practices

- **Industry Collaboration:** It is essential for collective effect to work with industry partners, academic institutions, and regulatory agencies to create best practices and standards for sustainability in machine learning.

- **Raising Awareness:** Systemic change within businesses and throughout the industry can be facilitated by educating stakeholders about the environmental impact of machine learning and encouraging sustainable practices.

Organizations may continue to develop in the ML area and help create a more sustainable future by addressing the environmental impact of industrial ML. Fostering long-term success in a society that is becoming more interconnected requires striking a balance between ethical and environmental obligations and technical innovation.

Managing moral and legal issues in machine learning is essential to creating responsible technologies that reduce risks and advance society. Organizations may promote trust and transparency in their machine learning endeavors by tackling prejudice and fairness, guaranteeing data privacy and compliance, and reducing environmental effects. This will ultimately help to create a more sustainable and equitable future.

CHAPTER 10

INDUSTRIALIZED MACHINE LEARNING'S FUTURE TRENDS

The field of industrialized machine learning (ML) is going through major changes as we enter a time of swift technological advancement. With an emphasis on three key areas the emergence of AI-as-a-Service and ML platforms, developments in explainable and reliable AI, and the future of human-AI collaboration this chapter examines the trends that will shape this field in the future. For firms hoping to responsibly and significantly utilize machine learning, it is imperative that they comprehend these developments.

10.1 The Development of ML Platforms and AI-as-a-Service

A paradigm shift in how businesses access and use machine learning technologies is represented by AI-as-a-Service (AIaaS). Businesses may implement, scale, and manage machine learning (ML) solutions by utilizing cloud-based platforms without requiring significant infrastructure investments or specialist knowledge.

Cost-Effective Solutions:

- **Accessibility and Scalability** With the pay-as-you-go approach offered by AIaaS platforms, businesses may access sophisticated machine learning capabilities without having to pay for the initial expenses of setting up and maintaining on-premises systems. Small and medium-sized businesses can now compete with larger organizations thanks to the democratization of access to AI technologies.

- The infrastructure is scalable. The ability to scale resources up or down in response to demand is provided by cloud-based platforms. This flexibility guarantees that businesses can effectively handle workloads without overcommitting resources, particularly during periods of high consumption.

Various Products

- **Pre-made Models and Tools:** Pre-trained models,

APIs, and development tools are frequently offered by AIaaS platforms, allowing businesses to swiftly deploy ML solutions that are customized to meet their unique requirements. Predictive analytics, image recognition, natural language processing, and other solutions are included in this.

- **Capabilities for Integration:** The adoption of ML across a range of corporate operations is made easier by the smooth connection that many AIaaS providers offer with current data systems and workflows. For AI-driven projects, this compatibility speeds up time-to-market and improves operational efficiency.

Encouraging Innovation

- **Pay Attention to Core Business:** Businesses can refocus their resources on innovation and essential business operations by contracting with AIaaS providers to handle their ML infrastructure and management. This change makes it possible to concentrate more on strategic projects, which raises market competitiveness.

- **Constant Improvements and Updates:** Regular upgrades and enhancements are often included in cloud-based AI services, guaranteeing that businesses take advantage of the most recent developments in machine learning technology. This ongoing development encourages innovation and keeps a competitive edge.

Difficulties and Things to Think About

- **Data Security and Privacy:** Data security and privacy are major concerns as businesses depend more and more on outside vendors for machine learning services. When choosing AIaaS partners, organizations must perform extensive due diligence to guarantee regulatory compliance and safeguard sensitive data.

- **Risks of Vendor Lock-In:** Dependency issues may arise from relying solely on one AIaaS provider. Organizations should create plans to reduce these risks, including using multi-cloud techniques or open-source solutions to preserve flexibility.

10.2 Developments in Trustworthy and Explainable AI

The requirement for AI models to be transparent and

interpretable has grown in importance as machine learning systems get more intricate. The goal of explainable AI (XAI) is to increase confidence and facilitate moral decision-making by making machine learning (ML) models easier for stakeholders and users to understand.

Importance of Explainability

- **Building Trust:** The broad use of AI technologies depends on trust. Explainable models help customers comprehend the reasoning behind predictions by offering insights into the decision-making process. Building trust with stakeholders and end users requires this transparency.

- **Compliance with Regulations:** Explainability in AI systems is starting to be required by a number of regulatory frameworks, especially in fields like criminal justice, healthcare, and finance. To prevent legal ramifications, organizations must make sure that their models adhere to these requirements.

Model-Agnostic Approaches:

- **Techniques for Explainable AI:** The predictions of different models, independent of their complexity, can be interpreted using methods like SHAP (SHapley Additive exPlanations) and LIME (Local Interpretable Model-agnostic Explanations). These methods assist in demythologizing black-box models and giving stakeholders insightful justifications.

- **Models that can be interpreted:** Certain machine learning methods, including linear regression and decision trees, are inherently interpretable. When explainability is a top concern, organizations may choose to use these models, even if doing so sometimes compromises performance.

Ethical Considerations:

- **Reliable AI Frameworks:** In order to ensure that models function in accordance with social values and conventions, organizations must set ethical rules for AI development and implementation. Addressing biases in training data and putting fairness mechanisms in place to stop prejudice are part of this.

- **Ongoing Observation:** Setting up monitoring systems and feedback loops is essential for evaluating the effectiveness and long-term effects of

AI models. This continuous assessment aids in locating possible problems with accountability, openness, and justice.

The Function of Stakeholders

- **Interdisciplinarity in Cooperation:** Data scientists, ethicists, legal professionals, and domain experts must work together to develop confidence in AI. A thorough grasp of the ramifications of AI systems is ensured by involving a variety of stakeholders in the development of AI.

- **Education of Users:** Fostering reasonable expectations requires educating end users about the potential and constraints of AI technologies. Giving people the tools and training they need can enable them to use AI insights to make wise decisions.

Organizations may cultivate a culture of accountability, transparency, and ethical responsibility in their machine learning endeavors by developing explainable and reliable AI, which will ultimately produce more socially responsible and sustainable results.

10.3 Human-AI Corporation's Future

A collaborative paradigm is emerging in the interaction between humans and machine learning systems, where AI enhances rather than replaces human abilities. The significance of promoting synergy between machine learning and human intelligence is highlighted by this trend.

Improving Human Decision-Making

- **Augmented Intelligence:** Machine learning systems can offer suggestions and insights that improve human decision-making. AI is able to make better informed and data-driven decisions by examining large datasets and finding patterns and trends that human analysts might not see right away.

- **Customization:** AI can improve user experiences by customizing services and recommendations to each user's tastes and requirements. For instance, ML systems can evaluate patient data in the healthcare industry to offer individualized interventions and treatment strategies.

Models for Collaboration

- **Human-in-the-Loop Systems:** Models are continuously improved based on feedback from the real world when human expertise is incorporated into the machine learning process. In high-stakes settings like healthcare and finance, where human judgment is essential for deciphering complex data, this method is especially beneficial.

- **Working together to create:** By involving end users in the development process, businesses can obtain insightful opinions and feedback that helps create AI products that are more applicable and easy to use. Co-creation raises the possibility of successful adoption and cultivates a sense of ownership.

Workforce development:

- **Training and upskilling:** Businesses must spend money on staff training and upskilling as AI systems proliferate. Maximizing the advantages of collaboration will require giving staff members the information and abilities they need to collaborate with AI technologies.

- **Multidisciplinary Groups:** The efficacy of AI projects can be increased by encouraging interdisciplinary cooperation among data scientists, subject matter experts, and other stakeholders. Diverse teams provide more creative ideas because they bring a range of viewpoints and skills to the table.

Ethical and Social Implications

- **Concerns about job displacement:** Ethical and Social Implications Although AI might enhance human abilities, there are worries that automation may result in job displacement. In order to solve these issues, organizations should prioritize reskilling programs and promote positions that call for human ingenuity and critical thinking.

- The concept of social responsibility Businesses need to think about the wider societal effects of their technologies as AI systems take a bigger role in society's decision-making. Collaboration between humans and AI should be encouraged since it is morally right and benefits society.

- Collaboration between humans and AI is expected to

open up new avenues for efficiency and creativity in the future. Organizations may leverage the advantages of both machine learning and human intelligence by adopting a collaborative attitude, which might have revolutionary effects on a variety of industries.

In conclusion, how businesses use AI technologies is about to change due to upcoming developments in industrialized machine learning. Navigating the intricacies of this changing environment will require embracing AI-as-a-Service, developing explainable and reliable AI, and encouraging human-AI collaboration. Organizations can promote good change and guarantee the responsible development of machine learning systems that benefit society at large by giving ethical issues top priority and encouraging innovation.

ABOUT THE AUTHOR

 Author and thought leader in the IT field Taylor Royce is well known. He has a two-decade career and is an expert at tech trend analysis and forecasting, which enables a wide audience to understand complicated concepts.

Royce's considerable involvement in the IT industry stemmed from his passion with technology, which he developed during his computer science studies. He has extensive knowledge of the industry because of his experience in both software development and strategic consulting.

Known for his research and lucidity, he has written multiple best-selling books and contributed to esteemed tech periodicals. Translations of Royce's books throughout the world demonstrate his impact.

Royce is a well-known authority on emerging technologies and their effects on society, frequently requested as a speaker at international conferences and as a guest on tech podcasts. He promotes the development of ethical technology, emphasizing problems like data privacy and the digital divide.

In addition, with a focus on sustainable industry growth, Royce mentors upcoming tech experts and supports IT education projects. Taylor Royce is well known for his ability to combine analytical thinking with technical know-how. He sees a time when technology will ethically benefit humanity.